This delightful book is the latest in the series of Ladybird books which have been specially planned to help grown-ups with the world about them.

As in the other books in this series, the large clear script, the careful choice of words, the frequent repetition and the thoughtful matching of text with pictures all enable grown-ups to think they have taught themselves to cope. The subject of the book will greatly appeal to grown-ups.

Series 999

THE LADYBIRD
BOOKS FOR GROWN–UPS SERIES

THE NEW YOU

by

J.A. HAZELEY, N.S.F.W. and J.P. MORRIS, O.M.G.

(Authors of 'Deliciously Earwax')

Publishers: Ladybird Books Ltd., Loughborough
Printed in England. If wet, Italy.

There may come a time in your life when you decide to make some changes.

You may wish to have a change of job. You may want to be a different shape. Or perhaps you are looking to pursue a new interest.

Jenna has taken up life-guards.

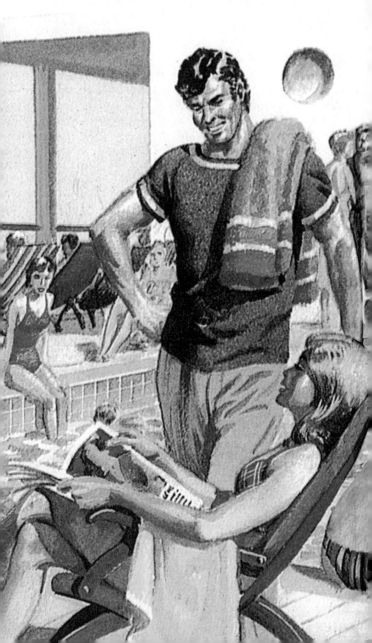

A new you could do anything.

Try a new hair-style. Take up candle-making. Learn the flute.

Maybe there is somewhere you have always wanted to visit.

The recipe on the website says that Johanna needs powdered cordyceps protein, ashwagandha, maca, coconut sugar, jicama, ho shou wu, bee bread and Reishi spore crystals.

She can't find any of them in Sainsbury's, but can buy all of them from the website where she found the recipe.

Prentis should probably have stuck to laps of the park.

He is due at work in twenty minutes.

Stella spent £190 on make-up designed to achieve that "no make-up" look.

She had a promo code for the website, so has saved herself £10 on looking as though she has spent nothing.

Spirit Freedream chose his new name after experiencing a neuro-hormonal awakening.

His previous name was Sir Alan Wood.

This may have an unfortunate bearing on the title of the parliamentary report he has been preparing on UK war crimes.

After realising he had a bad reaction to milk, Roger tried goat's milk, rice milk, soy milk, almond milk, flax milk, hazelnut milk, hemp milk, cashew milk, coconut milk, pea milk, potato milk, crab milk, garlic milk, wood milk and air milk.

He has given up trying and switched to Vanilla Frijj.

For her 45th birthday, Nicola treated herself to a £120 session with a 26-year-old life coach who gave her an ex-library copy of The Book On The Taboo Against Knowing Who You Are and some tips on how to get in touch with her inner life coach.

When Nicola phones to complain some weeks later, the life coach tells her that he is no longer a life coach.

He is now a change mentor.

It is easy to remember that some things are full of calories, and maybe refuse them when offered.

Cream cakes. Pats of butter. A haunch of fudge.

But a glass of wine with lunch or an ice-cream on a hot day are very different.

Those are not "real" calories and the human body definitely knows that.

The man running the course promised he could make Diane a new woman.

"Then how come animals don'
have problems?" says Neil to hi
Talking With Men group.

He thinks this is a very cleve
point. He read it somewhere.

It is not a clever point. It is som
words in the shape of a point
occupying the space where ther
could more usefully be a point, i
only Neil had thought of one.

Margaret thinks her colleagues at work are making a bit of a fuss.

It is just teeth-whitening.

"Of course you won't lose any weight on this exercise regime it's mainly upper—body strength" explains Sam's trainer.

Sam only joined the gym to lose some weight. This is apparently not something a gym can do.

Sam suspects the gym might be a secret club for people who like to watch Bargain Hunt and Frasier with the sound down.

Since she turned fruitarian, Cistine is feeling healthier and more energetic than ever.

Although she uses a lot of that energy sprinting to the toilet.

Gillibrand works for a Sunday magazine.

He is writing a column about how he is going for a whole year without giving anything up for the sake of a column.

George is at Fitness And Witness Camp, where he is doing daily Ayurvedic Kick—Boxing and High Intensity Impact Meditation.

He finds he is sleeping much better.

This is because he is absolutely exhausted all the time.

Gina has taken up rock–stacking. She has to balance stone upon stone, and it requires patience, accuracy and care.

And spending a lot of time on beaches.

After a messy divorce, Jareth bought a small flat and lots of new gadgets, including an Alexa.

He likes giving Alexa things to do.

Recently, Jareth met a new girl he likes. Her name is also Alexa.

Alexa cannot understand why Jareth will not invite her back to his flat. He cannot imagine the consequences if he did.

Sharon has resolved to eat more healthily. She has bought a spiralizer and is trying to cut down on her meat intake.

For supper tonight, she had Quorn on the quob with half a baked notato.

She is now enjoying a nice mug of hot broccolate.

Josh thought that signing up for a reality TV show called Let's Go Crusade would lead to lucrative personal appearances, a modelling career and a recording contract.

After three and a half weeks in the show's dungeon, right now he would settle for a night-shift in a haunted sewage works.

Duncan has spent the two years since separating from his ex–wife working out.

He tweets a selfie from the gym every day, with a message like "Swole AF #ripped".

He has nine Twitter followers. Even the corporate account for Holland and Barrett has unfollowed him.

Melvyn's wife Claire supported him every step of the way during his transitioning.

Now Melanie, as she is known, is far happier.

And Claire has realised that it was only Melvyn's rage and unhappiness that attracted her to him in the first place.

Gottfried and Melina are trying a paleo-style diet based on the idea that we share 90% of our DNA with horses.

It is awfully high in fibre.

"Buy some jade eggs for your yoni," Della's mother tells her.

"They'll make it so much more positive," she adds.

Della clicks the "buy" button.

In a few days, she will find out what a yoni is. Then the trouble will start.